Small Log Homes

© 2001 Roger Wade

Storybook Plans & Advice

Small Log Homes

Storybook Plans & Advice

Robbin Obomsawin

GIBBS-SMITH PUBLISHER

Salt Lake City

The information in this book is intended to motivate and enrich the reader's thinking. It is not a guide for building. The author and publisher bear no responsibility for the outcome resulting from practical application of any idea in this book.

Photos used on page 6 and 22, courtesy Star Hill Ranch and New West furniture; page 26, courtesy Candace Miller Architect, Gandy Peace Interior Design and Yellowstone Traditions; page 27, courtesy Jean Steinbrecher Architects and Whitevalley Log Homes; page 28 and 29, courtesy Jean Steinbrecher Architects and Unique Log and Timber Works; page 32, courtesy Beattie Interior Design and Yellowstone Traditions; pages 34 and 37, Mayfield residence, courtesy Montana Log Homes; page 36, Metler residence, courtesy Maple Island Log Homes; page 39, Norris residence, courtesy Garland Homes; page 41, Aldrich residence, courtesy Carolyn Campbell Interior Design; page 45, Holmes residence, courtesy Montana Log Homes.

Paperback Edition
16 15 14 13   5 4 3 2

Text © 2001 by Robbin Obomsawin
Photograph copyrights noted throughout

Published by
Gibbs Smith
P.O. Box 667
Layton, Utah 84041

1.800.835.4993 orders
www.gibbs-smith.com

Edited by Suzanne Taylor
Designed and produced by FORTHGEAR, Inc.
Printed and bound in China

Gibbs Smith books are printed on either recycled, 100% post-consumer waste, FSC-certified papers or on paper produced from sustainable PEFC-certified forest/controlled wood source. Learn more at www.pefc.org.

Library of Congress Cataloging-in-Publication Data

Obomsawin, Robbin, 1960-
Small log homes : storybook plans & advice / by Robbin Obomsawin.—1st ed.
  p. cm.
ISBN 978-1-58685-043-2 (hardcover)
ISBN 978-1-4236-3333-4 (paperback)
1. Log cabins—Designs and plans. I. Title.
NA8470 .O26 2001
728.7'3—dc21

00-012261

Contents

acknowledgments

Heartfelt thanks: To my husband, Jules, who faithfully props me up at my desk in the mornings so I appear to be alive, seeming to know when to feed and rehydrate me so I have the strength to go on. Jules's exceptional talent and work ethic in the log yard has turned many clients' wishes and dreams into reality. To Mom and Dad, who bailed me out of tough times more than once in life, and who, in spite of their hectic business schedules, took time to read this text to be sure that I would not embarrass myself. I will always be appreciative for their input and wisdom and for teaching me the importance of quality work. To my brother, Randy Whitman, for critiquing, questioning, and challenging me in business and in life. I hope we have a chance to do more, even if it is from our rocking chairs. To my aunt, Bonnie Swartz, who puts her life on hold anytime someone needs help; I truly appreciate her stopping her world for our family whenever an emergency arises. To my sister-in-law, Lizza Obomsawin, who helped and encouraged me to begin writing. To Jon Carnes, the artist's hand that took mighty ugly sketches and touched them with his magic pencil, bringing to life my design ideas. To my three boys, Jarred, Jasson, and Jimmy, who were raised by wolves because I was locked away in another world of designing the perfect log home—all 143 of them, every week announcing that "this one was it!" Five years later they still have the nerve to laugh at me when I tell them I have created our own log home, as each one of the designs in this book started out to be our own. To Suzanne Taylor, my editor, who did not laugh at me but supported me in creating a book of small log homes. She has made use of my compulsion to share with the world.

introduction

Since so much information has already been written about manufactured or milled methods, designs, and applications, much of this book focuses on the handcrafted style of log building and construction. These storybook camps and cottages are inspired by renewed interest in smaller, more practical log homes. They provide a starting point for some basic but classic plans, thoughtfully designed to help you develop and create a structure that will suit your personal style and match your vision of the perfect log home.

These plans are ideal for a starter or vacation home and the concepts are especially appropriate for empty nesters. Once you decide on the exact use of your log home, you will be able to adjust the designs to suit your needs and plan a more conservative and cost-effective project. For instance, if you intend to use the cabin only for weekends or one- to two-week holidays, a laundry room, formal dining space, or gourmet kitchen may not be necessary. Bedrooms could be designed smaller or used as shared spaces, such as bedroom/office or dining/living areas.

A good architect, engineer, designer, and/or local builder should be hired to make the most of your individual needs. They will help you to fit the structure to your site and provide you with the construction drawings and approvals necessary to meet local building codes and requirements.

A small log home that is a place to escape to yet welcomes others can be a magical, timeless treasure to be enjoyed by many generations.

Building
a Storybook Cottage

THE DREAM

LEAVING BEHIND A COMPLEX, HECTIC LIFESTYLE AND RETURNING TO A MUCH SIMPLER EXISTENCE IS THE IRREPRESSIBLE DREAM OF MANY. The dream come true: a small piece of pristine property in the middle of nowhere with fresh mountain air, crystal-clear water, and sun rays streaking through the treetops; a cozy log cabin built from materials offered by the land, using a few basic tools and decorated with comfortable hand-me-downs and yard-sale treasures. It would be a place to ponder the universe and one's place in it, to rejuvenate the soul.

THE REALITY

Building a log home can be either a labor of love or a bit of insanity. It is an orchestrated compromise to reach the goal of having a simpler home while incorporating modern-day gadgets, materials, and technologies. I have built and contracted handcrafted log homes for twenty years and have experienced the struggle of keeping a project in check both for myself and for my clients. I constantly receive requests from people who want a "simple, cheap cabin" with a hot tub, three master suites, four bathrooms, fiber optics, cable, an outdoor

(continued on page 5)

When planning your log home, consider adding a front porch as a way to increase living space. It can be a comfortable nook for enjoying the outdoors.

LOG-HOME BUILDING METHODS

Differences in how logs are shaped and stacked create two distinct groups of manufacturers: milled and handcrafted. Before making a decision, look at which style best suits you. The choices are many and depend only on your preference and budget.

Milled or Manufactured Log Homes

With this type of home, producers use mechanized sawmills, planers, and high-speed woodworking machinery to precut a log into a desired profile, producing uniformly cut logs without taper. The finished home can vary in appearance from one company to the next because of the variety of log profiles and corner styles that are available with today's technologies. Milled logs are sold in a variety of packages or kits. Manufacturers of milled log homes produce most of the log homes built in the United States.

People who want a log home that doesn't look like the cabins from long ago prefer the uniform look of a milled-log style. Its great advantage is that it can be produced and assembled faster than a handcrafted log home.

Handcrafted Log Homes

To handcrafting enthusiasts, nothing captures the authenticity of a log cabin better than this art form. It is a centuries-old form of log building that primarily utilizes handheld tools such as axes, chisels, and scribers. These standard tools and methods have not changed over hundreds of years, although some power-assisted tools—such as chain saws, electric sanders, grinders, and heavy equipment for moving the full-length logs—have been added to help speed up this detailed form of construction.

Because of the labor-intensive nature of the craft, fewer homes per year can be produced by a handcraft company than by a log-manufacturing operation. Unlike manufacturers, who form the logs in a uniform manner, handcrafters generally use full-length logs, retaining the natural shape of the tree. Each log is meticulously cut and shaped for one specific location in the log shell, which is usually assembled at the company's yard. The pieces are numbered, taken apart, then shipped to the homesite to be reassembled.

Handcrafted log homes tend to fit into three categories of cutting methods:

- full-scribed,
- hand-hewn dovetail, and
- full-round chinked styles.

Costs can vary depending upon the level of workmanship and complexity of design.

laser light display, and "oh, keep it under $100,000." These desires compromise a project, ending up with a home that has "sizzle and no beef." Creating a small log home can result in a realized dream if it is focused on simplicity.

My favorite projects are small yet classic camps and cottages built in the traditional way, using old-world style and craftsmanship. I strongly feel that even the simplest structure should be built to last for many decades, not built with substandard materials and methods that will cause the structure to deteriorate in a short amount of time. Construction materials and labor are expensive. However, the cost of a professional, quality job will save dollars for the client and waste from our landfills. Handcrafting homes is a labor of love for the professional builders who practice it.

MERGING DREAMS WITH REALITY

Building today is much more complicated than it was in the past, and the skill levels required for joinery vary from crude to very skilled and complex. For the do-it-yourselfer, the reality of building a small cottage or cabin will require considerable time, complete dedication, and hard work. Even the smallest project will not be small if you are unrealistic about what is involved.

For those who are determined to have their dream, I suggest working hard in the planning stages. Keep in mind that bigger is not always better, and simplicity is not always simple. Think quality, not quantity. Learn the art of being conservative. If you need direction, find a builder or contractor who will take time to advise you. However, don't expect a builder to hold your hand throughout the project. Do your homework. There are many books and plans on the market.

Often, the person who says "That will never happen to me" is the one to whom it all happens! It is the person who says "How hard can it be to build a log cabin? My brother-in-law and I easily built a picnic bench," who will most likely later be looking at a half-completed cabin rotting in the woods. Things brand new and shiny always look good; it is the test of time that proves a project. The cabins and cottages that I have seen successfully completed are those in which:

- enough time was allotted for planning, designing, and engineering;

- the owners took considerable time off from work to be involved; and

- professionals assisted in the basic "close-in" of the structure foundation, log shell, roof work, windows, and utilities.

Plan your whole project on paper first to work out the basic concepts. The detailed planning stage should be the most fun—but may be the most time consuming—of the whole project. Experienced builders, designers, and architects take months and sometimes even years to plan a project. Choose key areas where you have expertise to add creativity to the project. Submit completed plans and specifications to a subcontractor in order to receive a realistic idea of the total dollars needed to complete your project. Remember, if the bid is $150 to $250 per square foot in your area, don't deceive yourself by thinking it will only cost $75 to $100 per square foot for your project. Also note that local building codes, the complexity of novel designs, and the choices of materials in today's market can create challenges as well.

The best advice I can offer for your success is to work with a qualified and experienced professional. A master carpenter is the best bargain you will find. Looking back, I'm glad that I was fortunate enough to have had many seasoned builders looking out for me. After all, even I began building because Bob Vila made it look so easy. "How hard can it really be?"

© 2001 Roger Wade

Special Considerations
in Constructing a Handcrafted Log Building

HANDCRAFTED WHOLE-LOG CONSTRUCTION HAS EVOLVED INTO AN ART FORM THAT HAS BECOME VERY POPULAR for high-end rustic camps, estates, and commercial buildings—even small log homes. It is also one of the most expensive building methods. Designs often call for vaulted ceilings and complex angled rooflines. Other features that raise the cost of construction are 1 1/2-story fireplaces, tongue-and-groove ceilings, spiral staircases, hardwood floors, granite countertops, and log railings. Because of these extras, there are special considerations to address when constructing a handcrafted log home.

The first decision to make is whether to hire a general contractor and a master log builder to lead the project or to hire only a general contractor. The general contractor is in direct control of the integrity of the project. A first-rate contractor can complete a first-rate job when highly experienced subcontractors are chosen who best fit the scope of work. Hiring a contractor with a

The centuries-old method of handcrafting log structures requires years of work and training to master. Despite the advances of today's society, it is still a labor-intensive process.

solid background of training, years of experience in conventional construction, and experience in overseeing subcontractors are all necessary prerequisites. Keep in mind, however, that even though a contractor may have installed a milled or manufactured log package in the past, many aspects of handcrafting differ from other types of log construction.

Unless the general contractor has handcrafting experience, you may wish to consider also hiring a master log builder as a consultant for the project. The complicated joinery and skill level required for handcrafted construction is challenging and exciting, even to the most seasoned carpenter. It takes many years for a builder to perfect his skills and to develop enough of a well-rounded base of knowledge to become a master log builder. It is a form of building that only a select few have the patience and dedication to master. The end results in this specialized field of work will only be as good as the crafters with whom you choose to work. In the hands of an inexperienced builder, even the smallest project could end up becoming a nightmare, so it is important that you think this matter over carefully.

Windows and doors require a shrinkage space that can be hidden behind finish trim, which needs to move freely to allow for shrinkage.

11

WHAT TO EXPECT / LESSONS LEARNED

One of the biggest mistakes people make is designing too much home for the budget. A custom home is not inexpensive to build. Choosing the right log builder, designer, general contractor, or project manager is the key to a successful project. They cannot guess your budget or make an unrealistic budget magically work. Also remember that if one of the members of the team does not have your goal in mind, things can go wrong very quickly. You are just as responsible as the team you selected; don't expect others to do your homework.

A good designer, architect, engineer, or builder should provide you with an estimate of the general housing costs per square foot in your area. Also, ask a log builder with whom you would like to work for a general turnkey rate per square foot as a reference point to start estimating your budget. Log homes tend to cost one-third more than conventional homes, due to the vaulted ceilings, complex joinery, stonework, fireplaces, and extensive use of wood and other high-end materials typically requested by clients. Most of the construction costs are driven by the quality of finish work and materials you choose.

Building a roofline intersection where trusses, purlins, and log walls meet may appear to be a simple task, but it takes an experienced builder to make it clean-cut and well connected.

One of the first situations you will encounter will be log shrinkage because the contractor or builder will be working with the natural properties of logs. A mistake that can be made in building a log home is overlooking the shrinkage details. If you don't understand the importance and mechanics of shrinkage and compression, be sure you hire someone who does or this will easily become your most costly mistake. Contractors and subcontractors who brush off its importance and impact on a structure shouldn't be hired for the job. Grasping the concept of shrinkage is very simple for a good and caring craftsperson.

Another critical concern is the aspect of making custom cuts. In most cases, special allowances and custom cuts will be needed for windows, doors, chimneys, plumbing, intersecting conventional walls, in drift-pin areas, through-rod bolting, interior columns, stairs, trim, porch posts, kitchen cupboards, electrical cases in log walls, and vent pipes. These are all affected by the natural dynamics of the log walls' shrinkage.

It is common for many log handcrafters to reinstall the log shell on the owner's foundation. The log work should already have most final cuts made before reinstalling it on-site. This is not an area for the novice, greenhorn

Log walls are prepared for sheetrock dividing walls by cutting vertical channels into the logs, allowing the log wall to shrink around the sheetrock walls.

chain saw operator or general contractor to start making cuts to the work. Even though the job may look simple, there are special anti-kick tips, low-profile chains, carver bars, and professional-grade saws designed to enable these types of "plunge cuts" to be done with the chain saw.

It is well worth the cost of having a master log builder available to make special cuts where conventional construction will be joined to the log work. I have been on job sites where highly experienced general contractors have tried to make the connections themselves. In one instance, four men worked eight hours to cut out a flat surface in the wall logs for a small shower stall. The next day, I sent one of our crew members, a bona-fide master log builder, to the site to make cuts to accommodate a full-size shower stall and it only took one hour. The contractor hired our master log builder to make all cuts thereafter; he became the contractor's biggest bargain.

These are only a couple of the more common areas that should not be ignored. Failure to address these standard handcrafted-construction allowances can lead to very costly mistakes.

There are so many tricks of the trade—there's no sense spending your time and efforts reinventing the wheel. Do your homework by checking references until you find the right builder for the job.

Despite their labor-intensive process, hand-peeled logs are still common to a handcrafted structure and allow the logs to retain their natural shapes.

Small Log Homes with Big Ideas

THE IRREGULAR SURFACE STRUCTURE OF LOGS GIVES AN INFORMALITY TO LOG HOMES THAT SPARKS IMAGES OF THE RUGGED AND ROMANTIC TIMES OF A MUCH SIMPLER LIFE, like those experienced during trips with the family to the backwoods, lake, or mountaintop. The goal is to build a home that makes you feel as if you are always on vacation.

Smaller, cozier log homes not only evoke a sense of security but also respect nature by utilizing fewer resources. Building a log home that is low-maintenance, cost-effective, and respectful of our environment will affect not only us but generations to come.

One way to make sure your home meets these expectations is to collect and make a file of items that are important to you. Create a list of wishes and needs. This will direct your focus on the overall plan. You may need to revise your list periodically as you research and learn more about yourself and your needs. Your priorities may change, or you may have to reexamine your lifestyle and determine what you wish to retain as part of your family values. There will always be trade-offs that must be faced with an open mind and an occasional reality check. Photos and articles from books and magazines can help spark the imagination and help you make decisions.

This small log home's character incorporates large-home details, such as log rafter tails that cantilever under the roofline and a stone-faced foundation.

Design by Jean Steinbrecher

Right: Although only 24 feet by 20 feet, this cabin can be a comfortable weekend or holiday retreat. It is based on the Cranberry Cove plan on page 72.

Adding a wood stove, reproduction-style light fixture, and braided rug to this dining room captures the old-fashioned homestead feeling.

The simple construction details of this small cabin make it a timeless and functional design.

GREAT THINGS COME IN SMALL PACKAGES

A home that will retain your interest over the years should have elements of excitement, whimsy, or unexpected surprise. These can be seen in a hideaway nook and the warmth and feel of texture created by rhythm, pattern, and materials, such as in entry-hall tiles or diagonally laid floorboards. Adding a splash of color to kitchen cabinets or accent tiles can also create these. The whimsy or unexpected surprise may be the silhouette of leaves carved into a roofline's fascia board, twig art used as a focal point at an entry truss, or a bump-out sleeping bunk that adds depth and drama to the home's design. A design doesn't have to be unusual or expensive to be special. Simplicity can be in itself spectacular!

Designing a small log home is a series of trade-offs, especially if you are on a tight budget. Focus on the exact features you need so as not to become sidetracked. The floor plan is of utmost importance; the exterior will fall into place with some additional attention. If a single floor plan does not work for you, then take pieces of the plan that work and combine it with parts from other plans you like.

A simple four-corner rectangular log home is the most inexpensive to build, with the caveat that nothing is inexpensive in today's building market. Once you pass that basic four-corner structure, the more you will be paying for style over function. To intersect additional walls, ceilings, dormers, or bump-outs, there will be additional costs for labor and materials to create the space. Small structural details are often labor-intensive and add costs. If a builder tells you, "It won't cost much more," or "It doesn't take much more time," just remember that although this is what you want to hear, you shouldn't fool yourself. Ask for the bid in writing; or if you are in mid-construction, insist on a change order from your contractor or subcontractor before the work begins.

BUILDING CHARACTER ON THE EXTERIOR

The scale and proportion of the exterior architectural details can make or break a design. Texture, color, and rhythm are important parts of classic architecture. The exterior achieves its spirited character from the composition of elements such as its windows and doors, along with the use of log elements and various natural or more-conventional materials, bringing building techniques to a new level of art in construction. The art is in establishing continuity between the many materials utilized.

Generous overhangs and exposed log rafters make the roof appear to embrace the home and add protection for the walls and windows. Their oversized forms are more than ornamentation and a very important feature of all quality log homes. The log home's overall curb appeal is important not only for the resale of the home, but for making it look as if it is part of the natural habitat.

Quality materials in the roof system, foundation, and other structural components are most important in a long-lived structure. The technologies in these areas have very much improved over the years. It is important to study the choices of materials, their life expectancies, and buy the best your budget can afford. The "bones"—what you don't see—are actually the keys to producing a quality, structurally sound home. If you have to sacrifice for the sake of budget, it would be better to adjust the home's décor and interior wall finish. These can always be upgraded at a later time if you wish. But once the structure is completed, making any alterations to its foundation materials or construction is tantamount to starting over.

Far too many buyers are sold on how well a model home is decorated instead of on how well it is constructed. You must spend time to understand the mechanics of what you are purchasing so you are not disappointed with your finished home. This does not imply that you have to know how to build your home (unless you plan to do that), but that you know how to give meaningful input to the builder or contractor.

ROOMS TO LIVE IN

A warm home is one that is filled with the people and things we enjoy. Knowing the importance of family and friends, we make a place to entertain, a place to comfort and soothe the soul after a stressful day at work, or a place to catch up on the kids' school news and the status of the day's events.

The bedroom is reserved for quiet and relaxation. Although a bedroom is a private retreat, most of the time we spend there is with our eyes shut. This does not mean the bedroom is not an important consideration when selecting a floor plan. You may prefer a bedroom location on the first floor for convenience or necessity, while others may prefer an upstairs loft with a master suite that creates a private getaway, removed from the rest of the house.

Many cannot imagine a log home without a loft. It can be a place to tuck in another bedroom, an office or study, or a nook for curling up to read a book. The loft's possibilities are open to one's imagination. Do not get stuck on the idea that you must have a loft. If you don't have the budget for all the bells and whistles, you can create a very romantic and rustic log home without a loft. Some of the most charming log homes I have designed or visited have had no vaulted ceilings, fireplaces, or lofts, yet have still captured the magical feeling.

© 2001 Roger Wade

Creating a cabin that is cozy and inviting can be as individual as the interests of the people who own it. Things like fishing creels can set the stage for the log home's decor.

Sheetrock ceilings reflect more light and add contrast and drama to the pattern and rhythm of the traditional trusses and purlins.

EVERYTHING BUT THE KITCHEN SINK

The kitchen is the heart of the home. It is also a place where much space is unnecessarily wasted and costs can multiply. Take time to work out every detail in your design with your local kitchen and bath suppliers. (These suppliers often have designers on staff who can assist you with design details at no extra cost over the purchase price paid for the cabinets.)

Not all log-home plans need log walls in the kitchens. Some may choose not to cover up the log walls that they have already paid for and want to keep the logs exposed for their natural beauty. However, others may choose to build a less costly conventional wall for the kitchen or bath. The mix of log walls with more-conventional construction can be aesthetically pleasing and create a beautiful and striking contrast. When utilizing a conventional wall, you must address and pay attention to the attachment of cupboards, along with the special connections needed to join a conventional wall to a log wall, where one must allow for the natural properties of log shrinkage and compression.

I have seen some very creative ideas and alternatives to accommodate shrinkage details in the kitchen, such as building freestanding cabinetry as furniture to give a days-gone-by feel, or building homemade shelves for storage and covering them with fabric curtain fronts.

Freestanding furniture was designed for this kitchen, giving the home an old-time look and feel.

From a kitchen without log work or only a dash of log elements, to a kitchen loaded with log details— the options are endless even when designing the smallest log home.

KEEPING IT COOL

Enjoying morning coffee while relaxing with the newspaper or mingling with friends at a sunset dinner party are only two of the many wonderful ways to utilize a porch in style. Before air-conditioning was the norm, the best way to survive a hot summer day was to sip a glass of ice-cold lemonade and sit on the porch while the ceiling fans hummed. Ceiling fans not only keep you cool but also help keep the bugs at bay. Remember, when installing ceiling fans in areas exposed to the outdoors, purchase fans with sealed components and blades made from weather-resistant materials.

To create pleasant and comfortable surroundings for your new log home, use old-growth plants or add new ones to create a cool outdoor room or patio for the warm-weather months. Deciduous trees with seasonal foliage provide a canopy of shade in warmer weather, then become bare during the winter months when additional sunlight is welcome. Always allow for plenty of air circulation between your log home and the plantings.

© 2001 Roger Wade

A covered porch can increase the spaciousness of a log home by creating an outdoor room. This porch swing adds a touch of romance to an out-of-the-way nook under this covered porch.

© 2001 Ben Stechschulte

The details of this wraparound porch include a gazebo-style alcove and a mix of roof pitches and styles, with the center gable sheathed in birch bark. A short section of handrail "twig art" built in a free-form Adirondack style is incorporated into the design.

SHARING SPACES

Planning spaces that can be used for more than one activity can save floor space and heating costs. Ideas include:

- Using the office or study as a guest room;

- Transforming a tight loft into a hideaway nook for the grandchildren's sleepovers;

- Creating shared bedrooms for the children;

- Combining the living room, dining room, and kitchen in an open floor plan to make the space feel larger;

- Creating built-ins to make efficient use of small spaces;

- Building a bump-out dining nook or a kitchen-bar-style seating area instead of a formal dining room;

- Sharing bathrooms or building an outhouse (a great conversation piece that will surely entertain guests);

- Making full use of seasonal outdoor living spaces by using porches for additional dining, living, and sleeping spaces;

- Planning a small laundry adjacent to the kitchen so that it can also serve as a pantry and mudroom; or locating a closet in the kitchen that can accommodate a stackable washer and dryer; the same could be accomplished by installing a laundry unit in a bathroom closet.

This room is a great example of how to create shared spaces. Two double beds, along with a lounge area, make a comfortable guest suite or a child's dormitory-style room.

© 2001 Roger Wade

Shared spaces can be designed with efficiency

and still incorporate style and beauty.

STRETCH A BUDGET WITHOUT SACRIFICING STYLE

Be efficient. Wasted space costs money—to build and to maintain. Before you start building, think about how you and your family live. Consider long-range retirement plans or the driving time and accessibility of the home's location.

Invest in quality materials that will last: they will turn out to be more economical in the long run. Quality, not quantity, is key to your future. Quality never goes out of style.

Combine stock and custom items. Since many log-home components are primarily custom work, look for items off the shelf that complement them. Choose quality window treatments, hardware, and accessories. Don't be overwhelmed by the available choices. Remember, stay focused on your needs—a want is only an item on your wish list. If you get caught in the trap of living beyond your means, you may feel the stress of the house owning you instead of you owning the house.

Search flea markets and architectural salvage yards for special items such as mantels, sinks, cabinets, and wainscoting. (I know one homeowner who found a pedestal sink from 1947 in perfect condition with a four-dollar price tag.) One of the most rewarding gifts we can give to our surroundings is to recycle a discarded item for a brand-new use. Such treasures can also give the home a patina that makes it seem like it has been there forever.

© 2001 Maple Island Log Homes

If buying a picture-perfect property for your dream cabin is top priority for you, a smaller yet well-designed home could provide the balance your budget requires.

41

IT'S ALL IN THE DETAILS

The details of a home make it come alive; they reflect individuality and style. They can convert a humdrum home into a jewel where guests' faces light up when they enter the door. Details can be created by adding an eight-foot bear at the front door who extends his paw to greet and hold your guests' coats, or by adding a whimsical twig bench to sit on while removing boots and shoes. A dramatic light fixture that complements its space or an iron spiral-stair railing that contrasts with the log and stonework can add life as well.

However, adding character and incorporating special touches has a price. It may take additional time and budget, or it may be a matter of doing the things you can accomplish on your own with natural materials around you. Some incredible things can be done with minimal resources and creativity. Some areas that can benefit from great detail work are stairs, bathrooms, and closets.

Stairs in a home can be a focal point or can be tucked to the side, designed plainly, fulfilling only the purpose of getting from one

The detail in this dormer is reminiscent of a storybook cottage. Tongue-and-groove boards have long rows of uncut pegs that "stand proud." The gable peak is overlaid with dovetail and scallop-cut ends, and the maple-leaf cutout is backed with copper.

Sitting on a Colorado mountainside,

this 26-by-32-foot log shell

is welcoming and charming. Although

it is one of the smaller homes in this

area, the careful attention to design

gives this one a big feel.

45

floor to the next. There are endless choices of stairs, rail styles, and construction methods. If the stairs are not a focal point, then more-conventionally built stairs may be all you need. Whatever the purpose, stairs should flow with the plan's layout.

Bathrooms are often an area where you may be able to reconsider placement and efficient utilization of space. Be open-minded: tucking a tub or water closet into the sloping angle of a second-floor knee wall can create a romantic and cozy refuge.

I have seen and designed some very efficient closets. Closets that are well-thought-out and organized can easily fit two to three times as many items and are necessary to keep the small log home organized.

This lakefront home is packed with character. Twig-art balcony railings, leaf-cut fascia boards, porthole windows, and a stone-faced foundation illustrate fun, whimsy, and classic Adirondack architecture.

a Checklist
for Contracting
Log-Home Construction

A DO-IT-YOURSELF PROJECT CAN BE A REWARDING BUT CHALLENGING EXPERIENCE. To keep your project cost-effective and efficient, here are the ten most important tools you'll need if you are going to act as your own general contractor:

1. Time

Being a general contractor is a full-time job. It can take an experienced contractor up to six months working full time to complete an average-sized home. If you are acting as a contractor on weekends here and there, be realistic and know that your project will take much longer. The success of any general contractor is based on realistic expectations.

Allow plenty of time. Projects always take longer than you think, even for an experienced contractor. On average, clients contracting their own homes have taken two to five years to complete their projects.

2. Construction Drawings and Specifications

This is the part of the project that takes a lot of time and patience to prepare. An average home takes 1,000 hours of planning. There are only

It is a journey to create the right home that touches the heart and captures the soul.

2,080 work hours in a year, so six months of full-time planning is needed for a professional job. If you short yourself on planning, it will cost you time and money later.

Planning time can be spent figuring the most cost-effective and efficient construction methods. It adds to your up-front cost to have a draftsperson or architect put your ideas on paper, but the expense will pay for itself by eliminating wasted time and materials. Building a home with character demands plans that are well-thought-out.

Specifications are also an important part of a well-planned project. These are written descriptions of the work to be done (the scope of the work) and the materials to be used. Blueprints are the construction drawings. Together, specifications and blueprints comprise the construction documents and become part of the contracts with your subcontractors.

When applying for a construction loan, plans and specifications are part of the documents you must supply. Keep in mind that many lenders are wary of financing owner-contractors. To improve

Take time in the planning stages to incorporate special spaces--like this elegant staircase--that will put your personal stamp on the home. They will be the elements that give your home one-of-a-kind character.

© 2001 Rob Melnychuk

your chances of getting a loan, make sure all paperwork is complete, including all construction documents, specifications, budgets, subcontractor bids, and construction schedules. A well-presented project shows the loan officer you mean business.

3. Subcontracts, Lien Releases, and Change Orders

In fairness to both parties, and so there is no question as to who should do what, all agreements need to be put in writing. In general, the items listed in the subcontract are the above-mentioned construction documents. Standard contract forms for subcontractors can be purchased at office-supply stores. You can add your specific needs to these standard forms or ask an attorney to create a custom form. A signed agreement can be your best defense in the event of a dispute.

Signed lien releases prohibit subcontractors and suppliers from placing a lien on your home. Lenders often supply lien-release forms and require signed copies before each construction draw. Relentless tracking of paperwork is important for your protection and will ensure project efficiency.

This log home embodies old-world charm. The fascia-board details include a decorative pattern cut into the second layer of trim. On the roof, large plates of hand-cut natural slate cover a home generations can enjoy.

© 2001 bois de la combre noire

Change orders are written notices to alter the work being performed—for example, adding a window or using a different countertop material than originally specified. Change orders should always be in writing, indicating the cost or savings, and should be signed by both the owner and subcontractor.

4. Subcontractors

Think carefully before taking on any part of the project yourself, since the learning curve and your lack of experience may end up costing you more than hiring a skilled professional. Because material choices are many and specialized technical applications and skills are needed in each trade, it is wise to use contractors for your plumbing and electrical work, as well as for other specialties. Some jobs require specialized tools and experience, and some require a license.

Check references carefully. Spend a lot of time looking at a subcontractor's previous work. References will also help you to assess skill levels, quality of work, ability to complete work on time, and job-completion habits and attitudes. Good subcontractors can make a job easier and less stressful. Treat your subcontractors with respect; look out for their interests. Subcontractors are important keys to a successful project.

© 2001 bois de la combre noire

This bedroom sanctuary is a soothing space to take time out from a hectic day. The classic chink-style log home, with intersecting log purlins and full gable ends, is what many envision as the dream log home.

5. Organization and a Clean Job Site

More important than experience are organization skills. Make lists of tasks that need to be completed and refine and reorganize them periodically. Keeping track of bids, invoices, inspections, planning changes, specifications, and more, is demanding but it is an essential part of being a contractor.

Insist upon a clean job site. Sweep up daily and pick up debris and scraps as you work—require the same of others. Have trash cans placed in different spots on the site to encourage neatness.

6. Staying One Step Ahead

Think ahead for your subcontractors. Post up-to-date construction documents, schedules, and project changes at one designated area on the job site. Schedule the project with a steady pace. Starting and stopping a project can result in hidden costs that add up quickly. Continually review and analyze your project costs to keep your budget in check. An average day on the job requires making hundreds of choices, most of which involve money.

The natural appeal of these fascia boards and sod roof adds texture and interest. A beautiful triple fascia begins with a straight board on the underside. The second and third layers are each cut in a different pattern, capturing old-fashioned charm and craftsmanship.

© 2001 bois de la combre noire

7. A Calm and Cool Attitude

If you tend to have a short temper, general contracting may not be for you. A general contractor is a problem solver. A large part of your day will be spent ironing out unforeseen construction problems as well as dealing with frustrated subcontractors whose trades often overlap. A calm disposition and the ability to resolve problems is needed.

8. The Desire to Do a Top-Rate Job

Don't cut corners. Quality materials often take less time to install and look better than substandard products. Do the job right, even if it takes considerably more time. You will be proud of the end result.

9. Safety First

Have the proper tools or safety equipment for the job. Read manufacturers' instructions and safety warnings before using a new tool. Do not exceed the capacity of the tool. Keep the work area clean and uncluttered. Work in a well-lit area; be sure you have enough light to really see what you are doing. Children, pets, and visitors don't belong in an active work area. This can be dangerous and distracting, not only to the visitors but to you and your subcontractors.

10. Research and Do Your Homework

Magazines, books, videos, television, and the Internet offer plenty of advice and tips. Study each specific task before you start. Invest in quality tools. Remember, do what you are qualified and prepared to do, and hire out the rest.

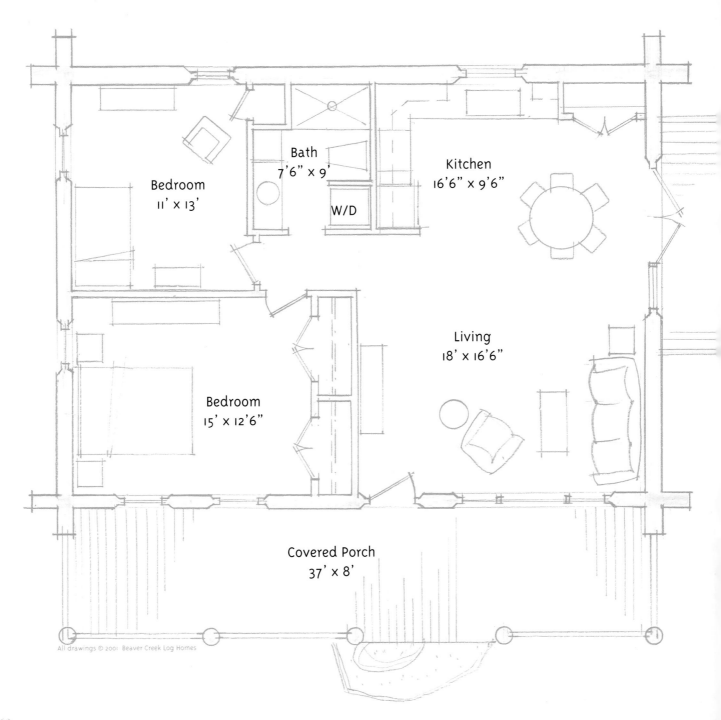

Bedroom
11' x 13'

Bath
7'6" x 9'

W/D

Kitchen
16'6" x 9'6"

Living
18' x 16'6"

Bedroom
15' x 12'6"

Covered Porch
37' x 8'

Clearwater *Run*

THIS IS A CLASSIC TWO-BEDROOM CAMP WITH VAULTED CEILINGS IN THE LIVING ROOM AND AN EAT-IN KITCHEN. Attached to the kitchen, a covered porch extends the eating area outdoors. Another shed-style covered porch runs the full length of the front of the home, creating additional outdoor living space and providing a fun place to sit during a cool summer rain.

The vaulted ceilings make this plan feel larger than its square footage indicates, especially in the great room. Since it is open to the kitchen, it allows for a larger space for comfortable gatherings.

With two bedrooms on the main floor, this is the perfect camp for a snug family nest or a weekend retreat.

The cabin's angled design is a visual treat reminiscent of camp days.

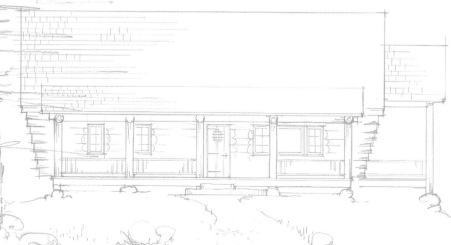

SQUARE FOOTAGE

First Floor: 1,064

Porch: 446

TOTAL: 1,510

Beaver Creek *Lodge*

THIS PLAN BOASTS A GREAT DEAL OF LOG DETAILING THAT CREATES AN ELEGANT YET COZY HOME. The wraparound porch adds an incredible amount of outdoor living space. If designed correctly, the log rafters, trusses, and purlins used in the ceiling's log work will appear to "dance."

The log detailing continues with a gazebo-style dining nook in the living area that is perfect for hosting a late-night game of cards by the fire. Guests can be tucked away in a ladder loft (not shown) above the master bedroom.

The kitchen has a rafter-style log roof system and conventionally framed walls. The kitchen walls can be sheathed in birch bark to flavor the home with classic Adirondack style. Two sides of the kitchen are wrapped in glass for a sunroom look and feel, bathing the room in natural light.

SQUARE FOOTAGE

First Floor: 1,250

Porch:............................1,028

TOTAL: 2,278

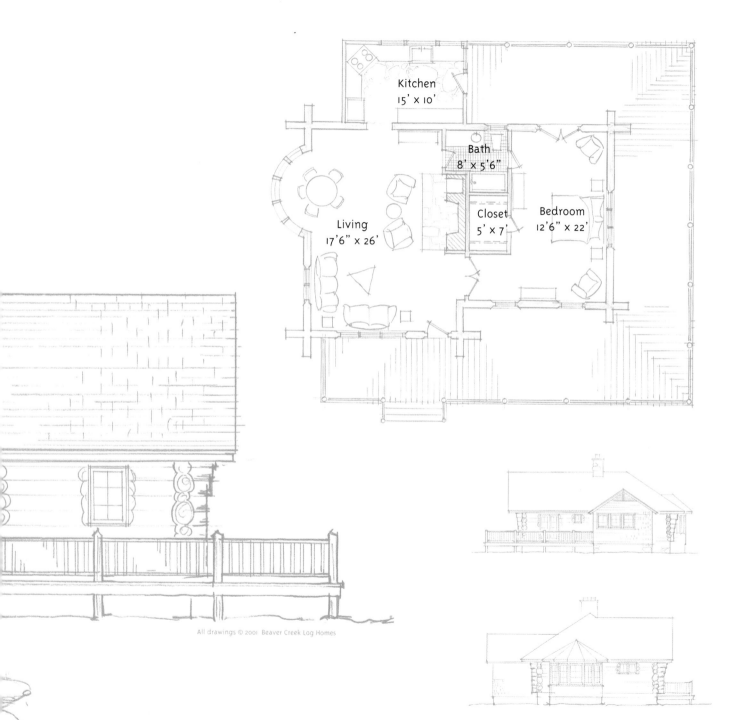

Kitchen
15' x 10'

Bath
8' x 5'6"

Living
17'6" x 26'

Closet
5' x 7'

Bedroom
12'6" x 22'

All drawings © 2001 Beaver Creek Log Homes

Norwich *Bluff*

THE COZY FRONT PORCH OF THIS HOME WELCOMES YOU INTO AN ENTRANCE HALL THAT GRACEFULLY opens up to ceilings that soar above the living and dining areas. A ladder loft (not shown) can be tucked above the bed and bath, creating a secret hideaway for kids. Walls of French doors open to a full-length back deck that doubles the square footage of entertaining space.

Much of the charm of this home is the sunroom feel of the elegant timberframe kitchen that sparkles even on the cloudiest days. Utilizing the centuries-old building methods of fully scribed log work and timberframe joinery can create a beautiful contrast. Using natural materials in a whimsical design on the front of the house enhances the wood structure's wholesome beauty.

All drawings © 2001 Beaver Creek Log Homes

SQUARE FOOTAGE

First Floor: 1,316

Porches: 794

TOTAL: 2,110

64

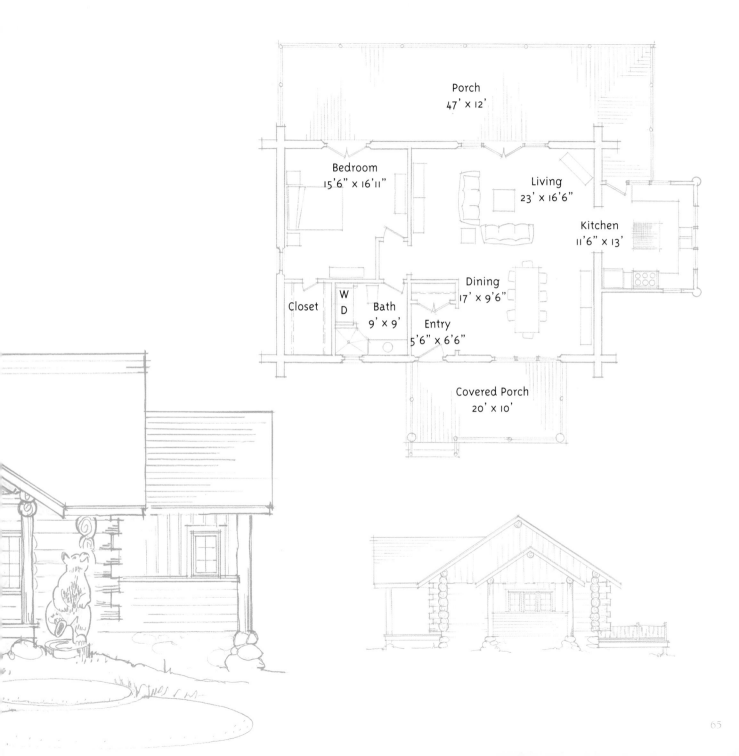

Porch
47' x 12'

Bedroom
15'6" x 16'11"

Living
23' x 16'6"

Kitchen
11'6" x 13'

Dining
17' x 9'6"

Closet

W
D

Bath
9' x 9'

Entry
5'6" x 6'6"

Covered Porch
20' x 10'

65

Wolf *Ridge*

All drawings © 2001 Beaver Creek Log Homes

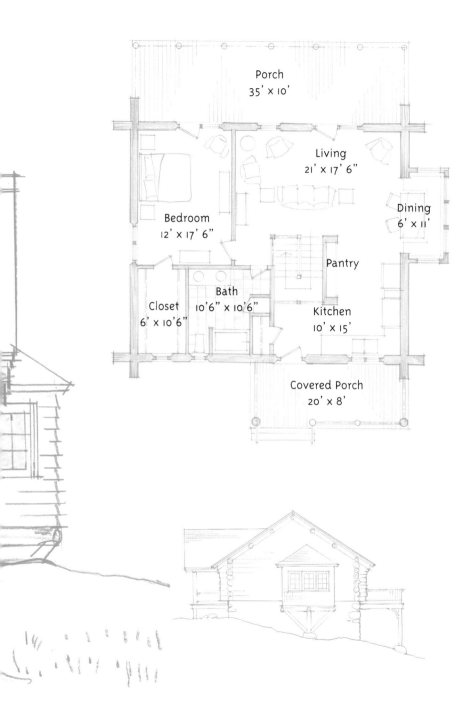

Porch
35' x 10'

Living
21' x 17' 6"

Bedroom
12' x 17' 6"

Dining
6' x 11'

Pantry

Closet
6' x 10'6"

Bath
10'6" x 10'6"

Kitchen
10' x 15'

Covered Porch
20' x 8'

ADDING A DAYLIGHT BASEMENT TO THIS ONE-BEDROOM RANCH WOULD DOUBLE ITS SIZE and create a spacious two- or three-bedroom home with a media room, laundry area, and garage (not shown) with ample storage. The bumped-out dining nook provides a wraparound view of the outdoors. The intricate ceiling soars and intersects the roof system, with a combination of whole-log rafters, purlins, and trusses. Without the basement, the floor plan still offers plenty of roomy options.

SQUARE FOOTAGE

First Floor: 1,170

Porches: 510

TOTAL: 1,680

Optional finished basement: additional 1,170

Caribou *Pass*

QUITE OFTEN, THIS IS THE DESIGN THAT PEOPLE THINK OF AS THE QUINTESSENTIAL LOG HOME. It captures the essence of a cozy cabin set deep in the woods. Its modest size still allows for an eat-in kitchen and a large storage area.

The bedroom loft (not shown) perches like an eagle's nest high above a spacious living room.

French doors off the great room lead to the deck, opening up a great space for entertaining or just enjoying the outdoors. They also ensure that plenty of light and air can fill the cabin when desired.

The screened-in front porch allows for insect-free evenings and storage for sports equipment and outerwear.

SQUARE FOOTAGE

First Floor: 728
Porch: 624
TOTAL: 1,352

All drawings © 2001 Beaver Creek Log Homes

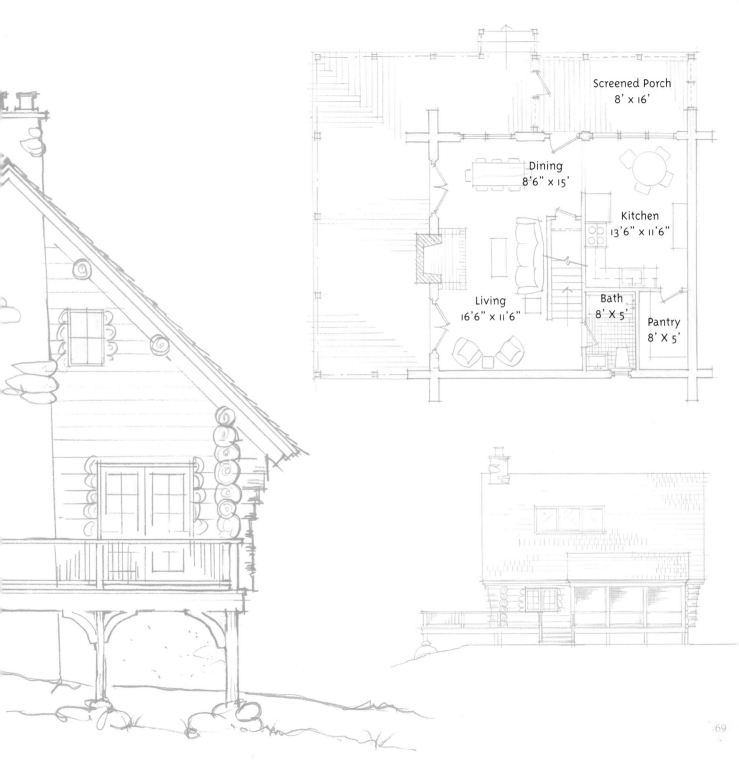

Screened Porch
8' x 16'

Dining
8'6" x 15'

Kitchen
13'6" x 11'6"

Living
16'6" x 11'6"

Bath
8' X 5'

Pantry
8' X 5'

Plum *Hollow*

THIS PLAN IS FOR A GETAWAY DESIGNED FOR FAMILY AND FRIENDS TO ENJOY. The spacious living room has multiple windows to make the outdoors an extension of the home. The side porch has a canopy of overhead intersecting logs, providing space for an outdoor living and dining area or a cool spot for a hot summer's sleep.

A second-floor loft (not shown), accessible from a ladder, is tucked away above the master bedroom, creating a magical place to hide. A full, daylight basement could be added for additional living space.

The bedroom incorporates a wall of windows into its design to add warmth and views. Two large closets, necessities for small log homes, are also accessible from the master bedroom.

The front porch allows ample room for sitting in a comfortable Adirondack chair.

SQUARE FOOTAGE

First Floor:.........................728
Porch:.............................624
TOTAL:........................1,352

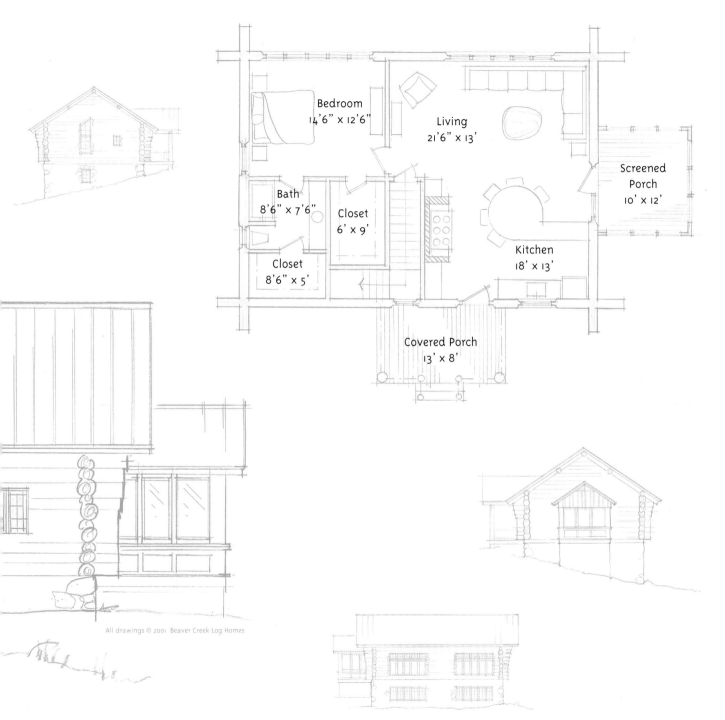

Bedroom
14'6" x 12'6"

Living
21'6" x 13'

Screened
Porch
10' x 12'

Bath
8'6" x 7'6"

Closet
6' x 9'

Closet
8'6" x 5'

Kitchen
18' x 13'

Covered Porch
13' x 8'

Cranberry *Cove*

AS A WEEKEND OR HOLIDAY GETAWAY,
THIS PLAN PROVIDES YOU WITH MUCH
LUXURY in a small, easy-to-maintain log
shell. This camp has the bare essentials and
requires few materials to build, enabling
you to own a camp without it owning you.

Resembling a prairie-like cottage, this tall,
narrow camp packs a lot of punch in a
small space. While humble in square
footage, the camp does not sacrifice
character on the exterior. The front-porch
details and river-rock chimney add flair to
the otherwise simple design.

Other details that enhance this plan are the
windows on the sides of the front door and
the front-door hinges.

All drawings © 2001 Beaver Creek Log Homes

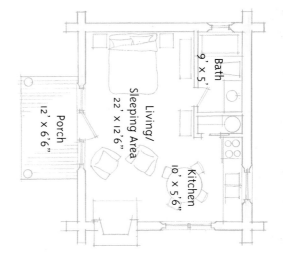

Porch
12' x 6'6"

Living/
Sleeping Area
22' x 12'6"

Bath
9' x 5'

Kitchen
10' x 5'6"

SQUARE FOOTAGE

First Floor: 480

Porch: 70

TOTAL: 558

The Weekender

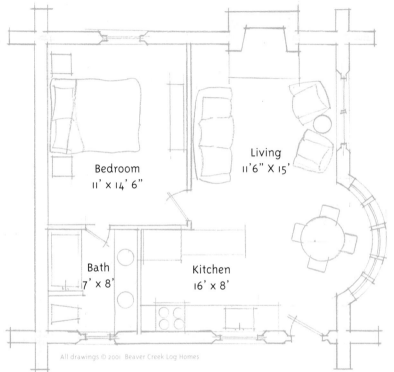

Bedroom
11' X 14' 6"

Living
11'6" X 15'

Bath
7' X 8'

Kitchen
16' X 8'

All drawings © 2001 Beaver Creek Log Homes

IDEAL FOR THE WEEKENDS AND HOLIDAYS, THIS CAMP COULD SLEEP FOUR WITH A FOLD-OUT SOFA.

Its design is an exercise in efficiency. This camp would be romantic with a fireplace or fitted with a picture window to capture the outdoor views. The hip-roof system is very impressive for its size. A complex design of log work overhead creates a rhythm all its own.

While its name boasts weekend use, this could be utilized as a seasonal retreat for a small family. The open kitchen, eating area, and living room add to its airy feeling and create inviting spaces to enjoy life's quieter pastimes.

SQUARE FOOTAGE

First Floor: 625

TOTAL: 625

Library/Office
15' x 12'

Open to Below

Bunkroom
15' x 14'

Bath
11' x 6'

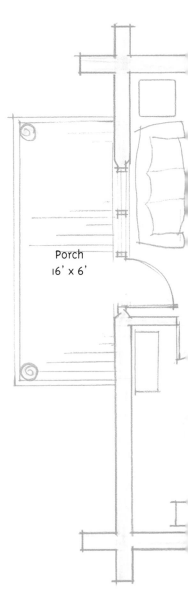

Porch
16' x 6'

Camp Dancing Bear

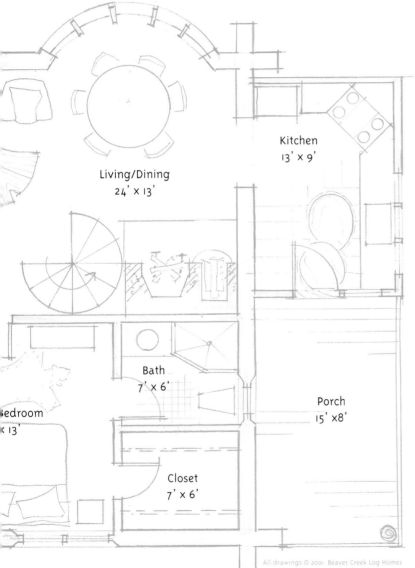

Living/Dining
24' x 13'

Kitchen
13' x 9'

Bath
7' x 6'

Porch
15' x8'

Bedroom
x 13'

Closet
7' x 6'

All drawings © 2001 Beaver Creek Log Homes

THIS LOG HOME IS DESIGNED WITH A WHIMSICAL FEEL. It has a variety of complex connections typically seen only in the old-world style of building. The compact size, coupled with the grand-scale use of log elements, creates a home that both surprises and inspires.

Some of the fun and unusual elements in this log home include a beaver-cut entrance column; free-form twig work woven into the covered entry truss; a gazebo-style dining nook; spiral staircase; a master bedroom suite with a walk-in closet; log rafters on the kitchen ceiling; and an additional upstairs bedroom suite, with a bumped-out Swedish-style bed, neighboring a loft/office and library with vaulted ceilings. All this detail adds to the charm of this plan.

The home explodes with personality.

SQUARE FOOTAGE

First Floor:	837
Second-floor Loft:	523
Porches:	216
TOTAL:	1,576

Corey Creek

MANY INTERSECTING LOG WALLS AND CEILINGS GIVE VISUAL INTEREST TO THIS HOME. A gracious entry welcomes friends and visitors then flows into the living area, where there is great interaction between the living/dining areas and large wraparound kitchen. The charming dining nook is cozy while capturing the light and views from all three sides.

Up the stairs, you can hide away in the window seat, located at the midway landing, to enjoy a rainy day, read a book, or talk with a friend in a place that feels like a childhood treehouse. The second-floor bedrooms have interesting angles in their walls and ceiling patterns. Back in the hallway you can climb a ladder to a secret loft tucked away above the second floor's log trusses.

The optional daylight basement is shown with an added guest suite or in-law apartment. It could also be used as a game room or media area with two additional bedrooms for your teenagers who may need more space away from Mom and Dad.

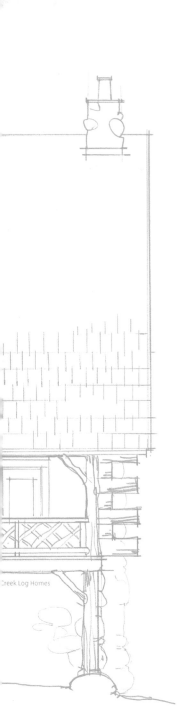

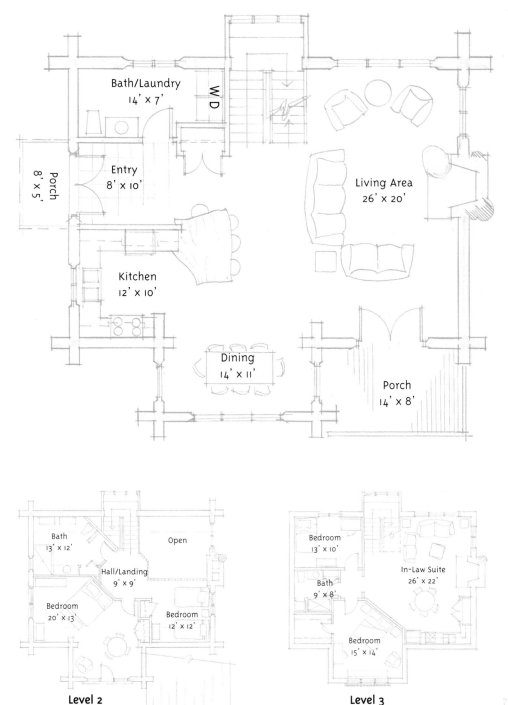

Bath/Laundry
14' × 7'

W D

Porch
8' × 5'

Entry
8' × 10'

Living Area
26' × 20'

Kitchen
12' × 10'

Dining
14' × 11'

Porch
14' × 8'

Bath
13' × 12'

Open

Hall/Landing
9' × 9'

Bedroom
20' × 13'

Bedroom
12' × 12'

Level 2

Bedroom
13' × 10'

In-Law Suite
26' × 22'

Bath
9' × 8'

Bedroom
15' × 14'

Level 3

Bayberry *Camp*

THIS HOME IS DESIGNED TO HAVE TEN-FOOT CEILINGS WITH MASSIVE OVERHEAD LOG BEAMS. Two covered porches with log trusses and purlins add additional log elements and character. The camp layout is efficient and cozy while providing a spacious living area for entertaining.

Note that the eat-in kitchen has plenty of cupboard space. Whether welcoming guests or accommodating family, this home does it with ease.

The larger covered porch off the kitchen adds an entire room onto the back of the house for playing cards, sleeping out, or enjoying an atmospheric meal.

With two bedrooms, increased living space, and ample closets, this plan could easily serve as a longer-term residence.

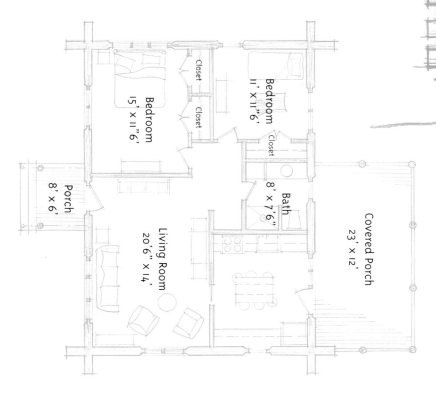

SQUARE FOOTAGE

First Floor: 1,064

Porches: 324

TOTAL: 1,388

All drawings © 2001 Beaver Creek Log Homes

79

Frog *Hollow*

YOU WON'T HAVE TO KISS A LOT OF FROGS TO CREATE THIS PRINCE OF A FLOOR PLAN. This is a home that has a warm and welcoming feel. The Scandinavian full-scribe-log structure's simple elegance is artfully crafted with a peaked covered porch directing visitors to the entry. A narrow back porch allows the low rays of the winter sun to stream directly into the house, while having just enough overhang to shade the house from direct intense sunlight during the summer.

A three-sided heated slate bench wraps around the masonry stove/fireplace with a built-in bread oven located in the large country-style kitchen. This type of heating system provides incredible heating and fuel efficiency.

This is a modest and conservative log home, but its jaw-dropping simplicity makes it a welcoming and comfortable place to be.

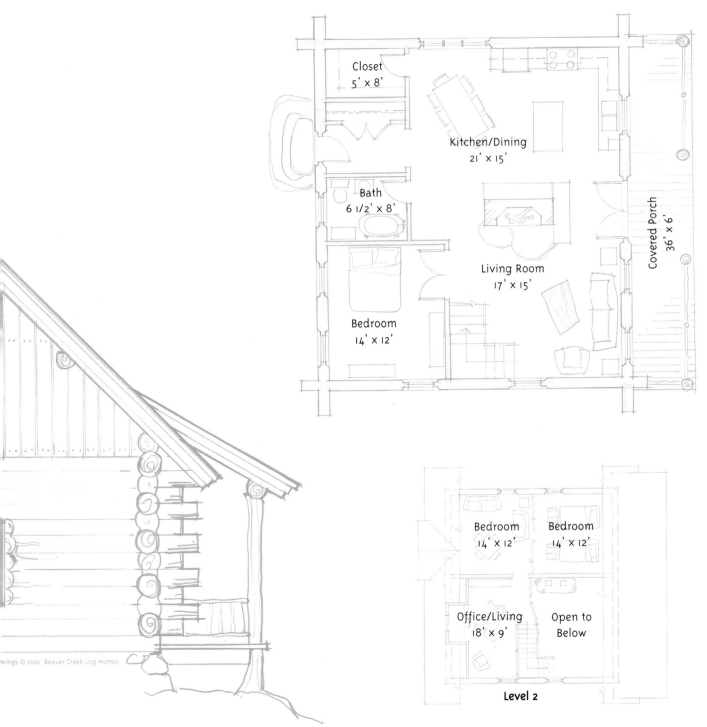

Closet
5' x 8'

Kitchen/Dining
21' x 15'

Bath
6 1/2' x 8'

Covered Porch
36' x 6'

Living Room
17' x 15'

Bedroom
14' x 12'

Bedroom
14' x 12'

Bedroom
14' x 12'

Office/Living
18' x 9'

Open to
Below

Level 2

81

Sundance *Lodge*

Level 2

Bed

Bed

Bed

Open

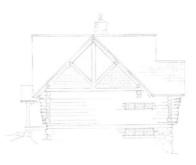

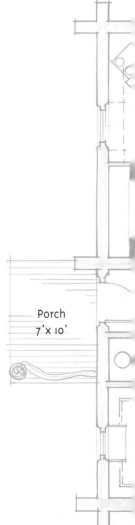

Porch
7'x 10'

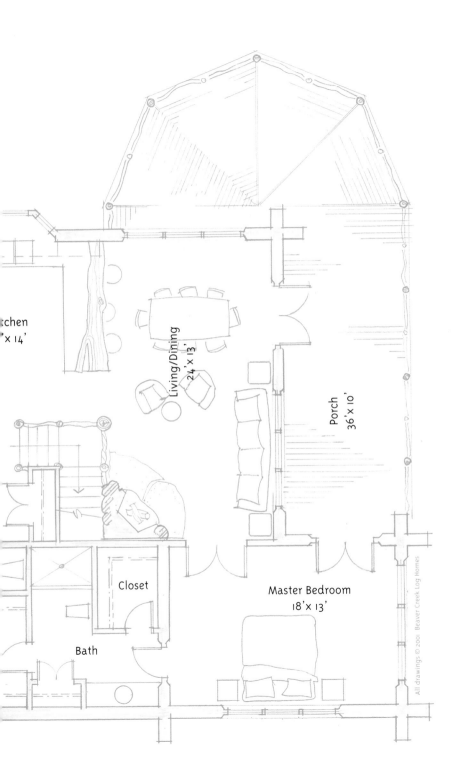

Kitchen
'x 14'

Living/Dining
24' x 13'

Porch
36' x 10'

Closet

Bath

Master Bedroom
18' x 13'

All drawings © 2001 Beaver Creek Log Homes

LIVING IN A LOG HOME IS LIKE BEING ON VACATION ALL THE TIME, HAVING YOUR OWN CALMING RETREAT AND A TOUCH OF THE FOREST INDOORS.

This is a home with clean simple lines and an overall open feel, with vaulted ceilings creating drama and interest. A little luxury goes a long way here.

The wraparound kitchen design is effective and well planned with plenty of storage, giving Dad plenty of space to cook those Sunday-morning breakfasts. The open floor plan provides a great place for snowed-in days of games, popcorn, and cocoa in front of the fire.

This log home truly makes the outdoors an extension of the living space, with plenty of covered porches for dining and lounging.

The steeply pitched roof and low gazebo-style porches give it curb appeal from any angle. From the interior, the rooflines of intersecting log work are stunning. This is the stuff that dreams are made of.

The Outhouse

IN TODAY'S MARKET, AN AVERAGE-SIZED BATHROOM CAN COST AS MUCH TO BUILD AS PURCHASING AN ECONOMY CAR. The outhouse—an important, though sometimes overlooked, structure—could be a useful addition to your cabin. This little building can alternatively be fitted out as a garden shed or similar outbuilding.

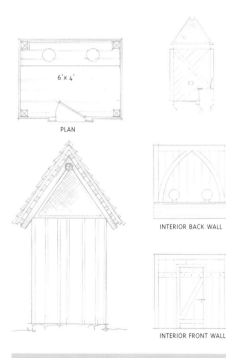

6' x 4'

PLAN

INTERIOR BACK WALL

INTERIOR FRONT WALL

All drawings © 2001 Beaver Creek Log Homes

SQUARE FOOTAGE

TOTAL: 24

Granny's *Cottage*

THIS STORYBOOK COTTAGE WITH
ITS CLASSIC LAYOUT IS A MAGICAL,
GINGERBREAD-STYLE COTTAGE your
grandchildren will always remember.
(No wonder the wolf disguised himself
as Granny.) A log ladder leads to a
"cottage-style" loft (not shown), which
can accommodate a weekend guest or
extra storage. The cottage is designed
with ample closet space and a large
pantry. An additional outdoor living and
dining area expands the living space.
The covered porch with ceiling fans will
keep you cool even on the hottest
summer days.

The kitchen is designed to have an
island with bar stools near the cooking
area, which creates a perfect area to
involve guests in conjuring up good-old
cabin cooking!

Covered Porch
10' x 4' 6"

Entry
5' x 6'

Bedroom
12' x 16'

Living
18' x 14'

Closet

Closet
5' x 7'

Kitchen
18' x 12' 6"

Pantry
8' x 9' 6"

Bath
9' 6" x 9' 6"

Covered Porch
23' x 12'

SQUARE FOOTAGE

First Floor: 1,064

Porches: 321

TOTAL: 1,385

Resources

Here are some of my favorite finds related to log building.

American/Canadian Log Builders'
Association International
P.O. Box 775
Lumby, BC V0E 2GO
Canada
(250) 547-8776
www.logassociation.org
An educational association for handcrafted-log
construction. Check their website for hand-
crafted log builders in your area.

Ashfield Stone Company
1739 Hawley Road
Ashfield, MA 01330
(413) 628-4773
Custom, unusual and artistic stone quarry.

Bear Necessities
by Hoppy Quick
Beaver Creek Log Homes
35 Territory Road
Oneida, NY 13421
(315) 245-4112
www.beavercreekloghomes.com
Realistic wood bear carvings.

Beaver Creek Construction Services
Designer Stock Blueprints
35 Territory Road
Oneida, NY 13421
(315) 245-4112
www.beavercreekloghomes.com
Designer stock prints of the log
homes featured in this book.

Bird Decorative Hardware
1081 Morrison Drive
P.O. Box 20429
Charleston, SC 29413
(888) 215-3883
Unique decorative hardware.

Bouvet
540 De Haro Street
San Francisco, CA 94107
(415) 864-0273
www.bouvet.com
European decorative hardware.

Chicago Old Telephone Co.
327 B. Carthage Street
Sanford, NC 27330
(800) 843-1320
www.chicagooldtelephone.com
Authentic old telephones.

Classic Gutter Systems
5621 East 'D.E.' Avenue
Kalamazoo, MI 49004
(616) 382-2700
www.classicgutters.com
Old-world styles of gutters and downspouts.

Designer Doors Inc.
283 Troy Street
River Falls, WI 54022
(800) 241-0525
www.designerdoors.com
Classic, traditional garage doors.

Good Time Stove Company
P.O. Box 306
Goshen, MA 01032
(888) 282-7506
www.goodtimestove.com
Specializes in antique heating
stoves and kitchen ranges.

Granite Lake Pottery, Inc.
30 Centre Street
Sullivan, NH 03445
(603) 847-9908
www.granitelakepottery.com
Handcrafted and hand-painted pottery
sinks made on the potter's wheel.

Heartland Appliances
1050 Fountain Street North
Cambridge, ON N3H 4R7
Canada
(800) 361-1517
www.heartlandappliances.com
Wood, electric, and gas stoves
with traditional charm.

Historic Housefitters Co.
509 Route 312
P.O. Box 26
Brewster, NY 10509
(800) 247-4111
www.historichousefitters.com
Period hardware, fixtures, and fittings.

Iverson Lodge Furniture
85 Maple Street
Shingleton, MI 49884
(906) 452-6370
www.iversonsnowshoe.com
Snowshoe style, steam bent furniture.

Jotul North America
400 Riverside Street
P.O. Box 1157
Portland, ME 04104
(207) 797-5912
Enameled wood and gas stoves.

Lee Valley Tools
1090 Morrison Drive
Ottawa, ON K2H 1C2
Canada
(800) 267-8735 (from the US)
(800) 267-8761 (from Canada)
www.leevalley.com
Fine woodworking tools.

Maine Wood Heat Company
254 Father Rasle Road
Norridgewock, ME 04957
(207) 696-5442
www.mainewoodheat.com
Masonry wood heaters,
cookstoves and ovens.

Murphy Rooms
16400 Southcenter Parkway #307
Seattle, WA 98188
(800) 488-3540
www.murphybed.com
Hideaway beds, desks,
entertainment centers, etc.

Reggio Register Company
20 Central Avenue
P.O. Box 511
Ayer, MA 01432
(978) 772-3493
www.reggioregister.com
Grilles and registers built in old-world style.

Rocky Mountain Hardware
1030 Airport Way
P.O. Box 4108
Hailey, ID 83333
(888) 788-2013
www.rockymountainhardware.com
Hardware for doors, baths, and cabinets.

Schroeder Log Home Supply, Inc.
34810 W. US Highway 2
P.O. Box 864
Grand Rapids, MN 55744
(218) 326-4434
www.loghelp.com
Specialty products for the log home.

Slatecraft
1796 Apple Valley Drive
Howard, OH 43028
(740) 393-1716
www.slatecraft.com
Slate switch plates and electrical covers.

Studio Steel, Inc.
159 New Milford Turnpike
New Preston, CT 06777
(860) 868-7305
www.studiosteel.com
Hand-wrought lighting.

Superior Clay Corporation
P.O. Box 352
Uhrichsville, OH 44683
(800) 848-6166
(740) 922-4122
www.rumford.com
Traditional clay chimney tops.

Tenonizer Technology
10480 Tenonizer Trail
Nisswa, MN 56468
(218) 829-9046
www.tenonizer.com
Instructional videos for making
log furniture and handrails.

Timber Framers Guild
P.O. Box 60
Becket, MA 01223
(888) 453-0879
www.tfguild.org
Promotes the centuries-old art
of timber framing.

Tremont Nail Company
8 Elm Street
Wareham, MA 02571
(800) 842-0560
www.tremontnail.com
Antique-styled steel nails.